HIS MERCY

endureth

FOREVER

~

psalm 136

ILLUSTRATED BY KATHLEEN DEJONG

REFORMED
FREE PUBLISHING
ASSOCIATION
Jenison, Michigan

Reformed Free Publishing Association
1894 Georgetown Center Drive
Jenison, Michigan 49428
rfpa.org
mail@rfpa.org
616-457-5970

Cover design by Erika Kiel
Illustrations by Kathleen DeJong
Interior design and typesetting by Katherine Lloyd, the DESK

ISBN: 978-1-944555-43-6
LCCN: 2018955197

*To everyone
who encouraged me*

O GIVE THANKS UNTO THE LORD; FOR HE IS GOOD:
FOR HIS MERCY ENDURETH FOR EVER.

O GIVE THANKS UNTO THE GOD OF GODS:
FOR HIS MERCY ENDURETH FOR EVER.

O GIVE THANKS TO THE LORD OF LORDS:
FOR HIS MERCY ENDURETH FOR EVER.

TO HIM WHO ALONE DOETH GREAT WONDERS:
FOR HIS MERCY ENDURETH FOR EVER.

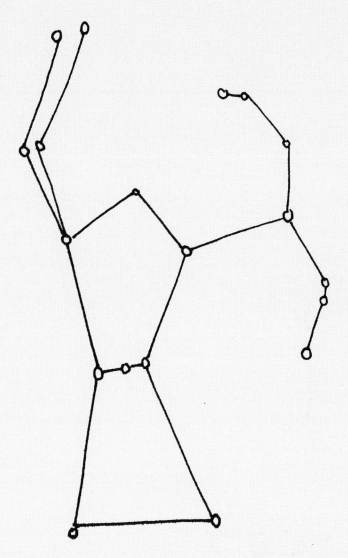

To him that by wisdom
made the heavens:
for his mercy endureth for ever.

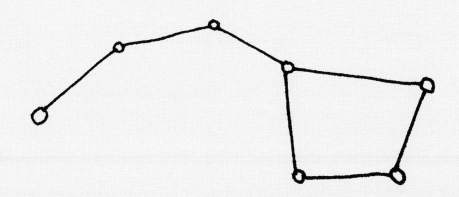

To him that stretched out
the earth above the waters:
for his mercy endureth for ever.

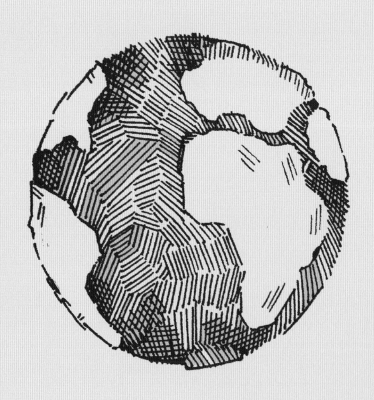

To him that made great lights:
for his mercy endureth for ever.

THE SUN TO RULE BY DAY:
FOR HIS MERCY ENDURETH FOR EVER.

THE MOON AND STARS TO RULE BY NIGHT:
FOR HIS MERCY ENDURETH FOR EVER.

To him that smote Egypt in their firstborn:
for his mercy endureth for ever:

And brought out Israel from among them:
for his mercy endureth for ever:

With a strong hand, and with a stretched out arm:
for his mercy endureth for ever.

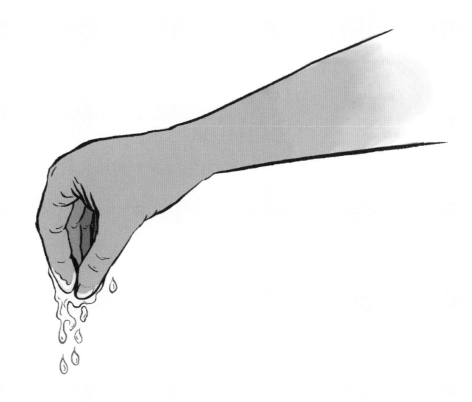

To him which divided the Red sea into parts:
for his mercy endureth for ever:

And made Israel to pass through the midst of it:
for his mercy endureth for ever:

But overthrew Pharaoh and his host in the Red sea:
for his mercy endureth for ever.

To him which led his people through the
wilderness: for his mercy endureth for ever.

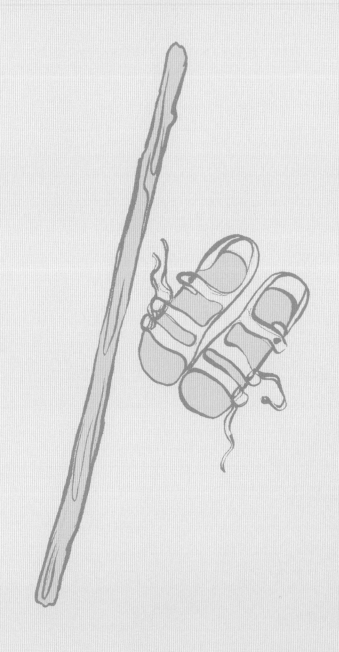

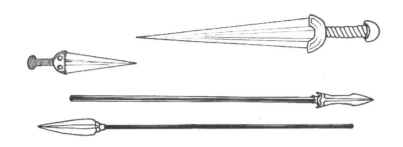

To him which smote great kings:
for his mercy endureth for ever:

And slew famous kings:
for his mercy endureth for ever:

Sihon king of the Amorites:
for his mercy endureth for ever:

And Og the king of Bashan:
for his mercy endureth for ever.

And gave their land for an heritage:
for his mercy endureth for ever:

Even an heritage unto Israel his servant:
for his mercy endureth for ever.

Who remembered us in our low estate:
for his mercy endureth for ever:

And hath redeemed us from our enemies:
for his mercy endureth for ever.

WHO GIVETH FOOD TO ALL FLESH:
FOR HIS MERCY ENDURETH FOR EVER.

O give thanks unto the God of heaven:
for his mercy endureth for ever.

Glossary

endureth—to last

firstborn—oldest child in a family

heritage—something that belongs to parents that they pass down to their children

low estate—the sadness of the people of Israel when they were slaves

mercy—God's love for us even though we don't deserve it

midst—the middle

overthrow—remove a leader by force

redeem—to set free

Sihon and Og—two kings whose people lived in Canaan before the people of Israel lived there

smote—strike someone or something down

the wilderness—the dry desert between Egypt and Canaan

wisdom—knowing the best thing to do or say